ABSOLUTE COMPOSITION

ABSOLUTE COMPOSITION

Structure, Threshold, and Transformation Across Forms

J. A. Gucci

Copyright

ABSOLUTE COMPOSITION

Printed in the United States of America.

First Edition.

ISBN: 979-8-9946751-9-9

Author Website: www.jagucci.com

Contents

Preface

Absolute Composition began as a structural approach to poetic composition grounded in compression, correspondence, triadic relation, and observable transformation.

The original framework proposed that meaning need not emerge primarily through symbolic substitution or interpretive abstraction. Instead, compositions could be organized through structural relations enacted directly within the work itself.

Early applications focused primarily on poetry: compressed systems constructed through threshold, pressure, transformation, and relational correspondence.

Subsequent compositional practice revealed that the framework extended beyond isolated poetic structures.

As the system evolved, thresholds were found to behave dynamically rather than statically. Pressure could accumulate gradually, disperse across interacting systems, recurse through repetition, remain unresolved, or transfer consequence beyond the originating structure.

At the same time, the framework proved capable of operating across multiple forms:
lyric poetry,

historical systems,
pedagogical structures,
dramatic performance,
recursive dialogue,
and cross-domain structural modeling.

These developments did not replace the original principles.
They emerged from them.

The foundational conditions of Absolute Composition remain unchanged:
compression,
observable relation,
structural correspondence,
threshold behavior,
and transformation through arrangement.

What expanded was the range of systems through which these principles could operate.

Part I of this volume presents the foundational theory of Absolute Composition as originally formulated.

Part II examines later developments that emerged through cross-form application and continued compositional experimentation, including:
behavioral thresholds,
structural lyricism,
historical modeling,
dramatic systems,
and cross-form structural integrity.

The purpose of the framework remains consistent throughout:
to examine how systems behave under pressure, how transformation emerges through relation, and how meaning may arise structurally through observable arrangement rather than imposed interpretation.

The emphasis is not on obscurity.

It is on structural clarity.

Reading Structurally

Absolute Composition approaches composition through observable relation rather than symbolic substitution.

The framework does not begin by asking:
What does this represent?

It asks:
How does this behave?

The emphasis therefore shifts from interpretation toward structure:
pressure,
relation,
threshold,
transformation,
distribution,
recursion,
containment,
and change across systems.

A composition within this framework is not organized primarily by theme, confession, symbolism, or narrative progression.

It is organized through structural behavior.

This does not eliminate meaning, emotion, or interpretation.

It changes the conditions through which they emerge.

Objects within the composition retain observable integrity.
Water remains water.
Ash remains ash.
A threshold remains a structural condition rather than a symbolic gesture.

Meaning emerges through arrangement and relation rather than imposed abstraction.

Because the framework operates structurally, it may extend across forms.

A compressed poem,
a lyric sequence,
a dramatic exchange,
a historical model,
or a pedagogical structure
may all operate according to similar governing principles if their internal relations remain behaviorally coherent.

The goal is not simplification.

The goal is structural legibility.

Readers approaching the framework may find it useful to observe:
where pressure accumulates,
where thresholds emerge,

how systems transform,
how boundaries contain or fail,
how repetition alters structure,
and how relations shift under duration or scale.

Interpretation remains possible.

But within Absolute Composition, interpretation
follows structure rather than preceding it.

The framework therefore asks the reader not only
to examine what a composition says,
but how its systems behave.

Part I

Foundational Principles of Absolute Composition

Chapter 1

What "Absolute" Means

The term absolute in this book refers to a compositional principle rather than a philosophical claim. It describes work in which structure carries meaning without relying on narrative program, symbolic substitution, or embedded metaphor.

In absolute music, a composition does not depend on an external story in order to function. The listener may experience imagery or emotional association, but those responses are not structurally required. The organization of sound—tension, repetition, variation, return—creates the experience.

Absolute Composition in poetry follows the same principle. The medium changes from sound to language, but the compositional idea remains consistent. Form is not decorative. It is the primary organizing force. The arrangement of elements generates meaning.

In this approach, a poem is constructed as a system. It is built around transformation, structural tension, and compression. The poem does not aim to explain an idea or illustrate a theme. Instead, it presents a process clearly enough that the structure itself becomes perceptible.

Metaphor is not excluded as a matter of preference or opposition. It is simply not used as a compositional tool. If a reader perceives metaphor, that perception belongs to the reader's interpretation. The poem itself functions without relying on symbolic comparison.

This book does not propose a replacement for other approaches to poetry. It documents a method that has been used consistently across a body of work and explains how that method operates. The goal is clarity. The chapters that follow describe the structural foundations of the system and show how those foundations translate into practice.

Chapter 2

Absolute Composition in Music and Poetry

The term absolute originates in music. Absolute music refers to compositions that operate without narrative program. The structure of sound—motif, harmony, modulation, return—carries the experience.

Poetry can function in the same way. Structure organizes perception without reliance on symbolic explanation.

The following musical examples clarify this parallel.

Beethoven: Motif and Development

Beethoven, Symphony No. 5 in C Minor, First Movement (1808)

The movement opens with a four-note motif. This motif does not describe an event. It does not represent a character. It is a structural unit.

The movement unfolds through:

Statement → Development → Recapitulation

The development section introduces tonal instability through modulation. The listener crosses harmonic thresholds before returning to the opening key.

Triadic mapping:

Motif / Harmonic tension / Return

The experience arises from transformation across tonal boundaries. No narrative explanation is required.

In poetry, an analogous structure appears as:

Initial state / Threshold / New state

The poem presents transformation. Structure generates meaning.

Bach: Polyphonic Structure

J.S. Bach, Fugue in C Minor (Well-Tempered Clavier)

A fugue introduces a subject, then layers additional voices. Each entrance increases structural density.

Triadic mapping:

Subject / Counterpoint / Convergence

The threshold occurs when multiple voices overlap and harmonic tension intensifies. The listener perceives complexity through relation rather than through narrative.

In Absolute Composition, a similar effect appears when matter, mind, and being operate simultaneously. The poem gains depth through structural layering rather than thematic expansion.

Debussy: Tonal Threshold

Claude Debussy, "Voiles" (1909)

This piece employs whole-tone scales that blur tonal center. Traditional harmonic resolution is suspended.

Triadic mapping:

Tonal clarity / Suspension / Dissolution

The threshold is tonal ambiguity. The music inhabits instability rather than resolving it conventionally.

In poetry, a threshold may likewise remain active without closure. The transformation is perceptible, but interpretive resolution is not imposed.

Structural Parallel

Across these examples, the following pattern recurs:

Music:

Tonic → Modulation → Return
Motif → Development → Recapitulation
Dissonance → Suspension → Release

Poetry:

State → Threshold → New state
Matter → Process → Being
Stability → Crossing → Condition

In both mediums:

- Tension arises from structural change.
- Threshold marks transformation.
- Return or alteration follows.
- Meaning emerges from organization.

Absolute Composition in poetry does not imitate musical imagery. It shares compositional logic with absolute music.

Structure precedes interpretation.

The experience is constructed rather than narrated.

Why This Placement Matters

Placing this chapter early establishes that Absolute Composition is not a rejection of lyric tradition but a parallel structural discipline. The comparison situates the method historically and aesthetically without polemic.

From this foundation, the remaining chapters move into technical articulation: triad, threshold, registers, compression.

Chapter 3

The Paradox Triad

A central structural element in Absolute Composition is the paradox triad. The triad is not a theme or a slogan. It is a set of three related conditions that generate tension within a system.

Many observable processes can be described in terms of three states. For example, matter may appear as gas, liquid, and solid. A seed may be sealed, activated, and opened. A surface may be clear, patterned, and opaque. These sequences are not symbolic; they describe actual conditions within a transformation.

A triad becomes structurally useful when the relationship among the three elements produces tension. Two states often create opposition. Three states introduce instability. With three, one element can mediate or disrupt the other two. This arrangement prevents simple balance and creates movement.

In practice, the triad often reflects a transformation across a threshold. There is a condition before the threshold, a crossing point, and a condition after the threshold. The middle term may represent a process, a catalyst, or a boundary. Its role is not to resolve the system but to hold the tension between states.

For example, in frost formation, the scientific description might include gas, liquid, and solid. Structurally, the poem may compress this sequence. The visible transformation from vapor to crystal highlights the threshold where one state becomes another. The triad provides an underlying structure for organizing that movement, even if the terms themselves do not appear in the poem.

The triad does not need to be named within the text. It operates as a compositional framework. It helps determine sequence, emphasis, and compression. It guides decisions about what belongs in the poem and what does not.

Because the triad is grounded in real systems, it remains stable. Its tension comes from the observable transformation it describes. The poem traces that tension rather than explaining it.

The paradox in a triad does not depend on contradiction in the abstract. It emerges from the fact that one condition becomes another across a threshold. The system changes state. The triad captures that change in a compact structural form.

In this way, the paradox triad serves as the horizontal axis of the poem. It organizes movement across time or condition.

In the next chapter, the vertical dimension of the poem will be examined through the three perceptual registers: matter, mind, and being.

Chapter 4

Matter, Mind, Being

In addition to the paradox triad, Absolute Composition relies on three perceptual registers: matter, mind, and being. These registers help organize how a poem presents a system across layers of experience.

They are not metaphysical categories. They are compositional distinctions. Each register performs a different function within the structure of the poem.

Matter refers to the physical and observable aspects of a system. It includes what can be seen, heard, measured, or verified. Ice cracking, frost forming, a cone sealed in resin, a branch splitting under weight—these belong to the register of matter. This register anchors the poem in the physical world and establishes credibility in the transformation being described.

Mind refers to pattern, process, and system. It includes movement, mechanism, recurrence, and relation. In frost formation, mind involves the phase transition and the conditions that allow vapor to crystallize. In a seed cone opened by fire, mind includes the activation condition that makes release possible. Mind does not introduce commentary or emotion; it introduces structure within the system.

Being refers to the state that remains after transformation. It is not explanation or summary. It is the condition that exists once the threshold has been crossed. A window that is no longer transparent. A cone that has opened. A surface that has changed texture. Being marks the presence of the new state.

When these registers operate together, the poem gains depth without requiring metaphor. Matter establishes what is happening. Mind clarifies how it happens. Being shows what remains.

The registers often appear across separate lines or stanzas, but they do not need to be labeled. Their distinction becomes evident through function. If all lines describe only surface detail, the poem may feel static. If all lines focus on process, the poem may feel analytical. If all lines emphasize outcome, the poem may feel abstract. The interaction of the three registers creates dimensional balance.

The paradox triad organizes movement across conditions. The registers organize perception within those conditions. Together, they create both horizontal and vertical structure.

Chapter 5

Three Orbitals of Compression

Absolute Composition depends on compression. Compression does not refer simply to brevity. It refers to density. A compressed poem contains only the elements necessary for the transformation it presents.

Compression operates in three related orbitals: image compression, structural compression, and conceptual compression. Each orbital reduces excess while preserving tension.

Image compression concerns selection. A physical system contains many details, but only some contribute to the structural threshold. In frost formation, temperature readings, weather conditions, and surrounding scenery may be accurate, but they do not all increase tension. Image compression narrows attention to the elements that make the transformation perceptible. The result is clarity rather than decoration.

Structural compression concerns constraint. Limiting the number of lines, stanzas, or repeated elements increases pressure within the poem. When the available space is defined, each line carries greater weight. Constraint does not restrict creativity; it sharpens it. Structural compression prevents the poem from expanding beyond the threshold it is meant to trace.

Conceptual compression concerns explanation. A transformation can be analyzed in detail, but analysis is not the aim of the poem. Conceptual compression allows the system to appear without commentary. The poem shows the crossing of the threshold and the resulting state. Interpretation remains available to the reader, but it is not supplied inside the structure.

These orbitals reinforce one another. Image compression reduces surface material. Structural compression limits expansion. Conceptual compression preserves tension. Together, they create density without obscurity.

A compressed poem remains clear in what it presents. The physical system is identifiable. The threshold is perceptible. The change in condition is evident. What is absent is unnecessary elaboration.

When compression is effective, the poem feels complete rather than abbreviated. Nothing essential has been removed. Nothing extraneous remains.

With the paradox triad and the three perceptual registers in place, compression ensures that the transformation holds its shape.

Chapter 6

From Observation to Poem

In this method, a poem develops from close attention to a physical transformation. The starting point is not a theme or an emotion, but a system that can be observed and described accurately.

The process often begins by identifying a change in state. What was present before the transformation, and what is present after it? In frost formation, water vapor in the air becomes solid crystal on glass. In a sealed pine cone exposed to fire, heat activates release. In each case, a condition shifts across a threshold.

Establishing the initial and resulting states provides direction. The poem traces the movement from one condition to another. This movement is not symbolic; it is structural.

Once the endpoints are clear, attention turns to the threshold. The threshold marks the boundary where one state becomes another. In frost, the threshold is the phase transition from vapor to crystal. Before the threshold, moisture exists as dispersed gas. After it, the same substance exists as structured solid. The crossing of that boundary generates tension.

Within this transition, a triadic structure often becomes visible. The scientific description may include three related conditions—gas, liquid, solid —even if one is not visibly present. Structurally, the poem may compress this sequence to emphasize the threshold itself. The triad guides the organization of the poem even when it is not named directly.

Drafting begins with the physical system. The poem presents the observable elements of the transformation: surface, temperature, pressure, release, fracture, expansion. The language remains grounded in what can be verified. The transformation unfolds across the lines.

During revision, compression sharpens the structure. Details that do not contribute to the threshold are removed. Explanatory language tends to fall away. What remains is the crossing from one state to another and the condition that follows.

In some cases, the physical system shares a structural pattern with a psychological or relational one. That correspondence may inform the title or remain implicit. The poem does not depend on the comparison in order to function. The observable system is sufficient.

A poem reaches completion when the transformation is clear, the threshold remains perceptible, and the structural tension has not been diffused. At that point, the composition holds its shape.

Chapter 7

Revision and Structural Integrity

Revision in Absolute Composition focuses on maintaining structural clarity. The purpose of revision is not to embellish the poem, but to ensure that the transformation remains intact and that the threshold is perceptible.

The first question during revision concerns the transformation itself. Is the movement from one state to another clear? The reader should be able to recognize that a condition has shifted. If the initial state is vague, or if the resulting state is indistinct, the structural arc weakens. Clarifying the endpoints often strengthens the entire poem.

The next consideration is the threshold. The crossing from one state to another should remain visible within the structure. If additional language has softened or obscured that crossing, compression may restore its sharpness. The threshold does not need to be explained, but it should be traceable.

Attention then turns to the paradox triad. Even when the triad is not explicitly named, its tension should still organize the poem. During revision, it is useful to ask whether the three related conditions are still active. If one has faded or been overshadowed by descriptive detail, the balance may shift toward explanation rather than structure.

The three perceptual registers—matter, mind, and being—also benefit from review. If every line describes only surface detail, the poem may lack dimensional depth. If process dominates, the poem may become analytical. If outcome is emphasized too heavily, the threshold may feel distant. Revision often involves redistributing emphasis so that each register remains distinct.

Compression plays a central role at this stage. Image compression reduces excess description. Structural compression maintains constraint. Conceptual compression removes commentary that the observable system already conveys. Revision frequently consists of subtraction rather than addition.

Finally, structural integrity depends on proportion. The length of the poem, the placement of lines, and the rhythm of the transformation all influence how the threshold is experienced. If the crossing occurs too quickly, tension may dissipate. If it is delayed excessively, clarity may diminish. Revision adjusts pacing so that the transformation feels inevitable rather than abrupt.

A poem is structurally complete when the transformation is evident, the threshold is present, and no element distracts from the movement across states. At that point, revision no longer strengthens the structure. The poem holds.

Chapter 8

Classroom Application

Absolute Composition can be adapted across grade levels because it begins with observation and structure rather than abstraction. The method emphasizes transformation, threshold, and compression—concepts that can be introduced in progressively more complex ways.
The goal in a classroom setting is not to replicate a finished style, but to help students recognize how systems change state and how structure can organize that change.

Middle School

At the middle school level, students can begin to identify thresholds more precisely. Scientific vocabulary such as phase change, activation, or pressure can be incorporated where appropriate.

Students may work with simple triads drawn from observable systems:

Seed / Soil / Sprout
Liquid / Freeze / Solid
Calm / Wind / Wave

The triad is not treated as a theme but as a structural guide. Students can be asked to write a poem that traces a system across its threshold while remaining grounded in physical detail.

Revision exercises may focus on compression. Students can compare an initial draft with a shortened version to see how removing explanation increases clarity.

High School

At the high school level, the structural aspects of the method can be made explicit. Students can analyze how a poem organizes transformation across a threshold and how the paradox triad creates tension.

Assignments might include:

- Identifying the "was" and "is" in a chosen system.
- Locating the threshold within that system.
- Drafting a poem that presents the transformation without commentary.
- Revising for structural compression.

Students at this level can also explore structural correspondence, noticing when two different systems share a similar pattern of change. The correspondence remains structural rather than comparative.

University Level

At the university level, Absolute Composition can function as both creative practice and analytical framework.

Students can examine:

- How thresholds operate across disciplines (chemistry, physics, ecology, psychology).
- How triadic structures create instability.
- How compression influences interpretation.

Workshops can focus on revision as structural refinement. Rather than asking what a poem "means," discussion may center on whether the transformation is perceptible and whether the threshold remains intact.

This approach encourages close reading of systems rather than interpretation of symbols. It invites students to treat composition as construction.

Assessment

Assessment in this method emphasizes structural clarity rather than thematic interpretation. A poem can be evaluated by asking:

- Is the transformation clear?
- Is the threshold perceptible?
- Does the structure hold across revision?
- Has compression strengthened or weakened the system?

Because the method is grounded in observable processes, evaluation can remain concrete. Absolute Composition offers students a disciplined way to see change, trace structure, and construct meaning through form. It does not replace other approaches to poetry. It provides an additional framework that emphasizes attention, accuracy, and structural awareness.

Chapter 9

Concluding Notes on Practice

Absolute Composition is a method of constructing poetry through transformation, threshold, and compression. It begins with observable systems and builds structure from state change rather than from theme or narrative.

The paradox triad provides tension.
The registers of matter, mind, and being provide dimensional depth.
The orbitals of compression ensure density without obscurity.

Together, these elements form a repeatable compositional framework.

This method does not eliminate interpretation. It separates construction from interpretation. The poem is built as a system. The reader encounters that system and may derive meaning from it. The structure does not dictate response.

Because Absolute Composition is grounded in real processes, it can intersect naturally with scientific, ecological, psychological, and relational systems. The emphasis remains structural. A transformation across a threshold becomes the central organizing principle.

Over time, variations emerge. Some poems may foreground correspondence between physical and psychological systems. Others may remain entirely within observable phenomena. Some may emphasize triadic balance; others may intensify a single threshold. The foundation remains consistent.

The purpose of this book has been to clarify how the method operates. The principles described here are not prescriptive rules but structural tendencies. When transformation is clear, the threshold is perceptible, and compression has removed excess, the composition holds.

PART II

Threshold Behavior, Structural Systems, and Cross-Form Composition

Note on the Expanded Edition

The chapters in Part II reflect developments that emerged through later compositional practice and cross-form application.

These additions extend the original framework without replacing its foundational principles.

The core conditions of Absolute Composition remain:
compression,
structural correspondence,
observable relation,
threshold behavior,
and transformation through arrangement.

Chapter 10

Introduction to the Expanded Framework

The original formulation of Absolute Composition established a structural method grounded in compression, correspondence, transformation, and triadic relation.

Subsequent works demonstrated that these principles extend beyond isolated poetic structures.

As the system evolved, thresholds were found not only to mark transformation, but to behave dynamically across systems. Pressure could accumulate gradually, transfer between structures, recurse through repetition, disperse across fields, or remain unresolved. Systems could stabilize, fracture, loop, invert, collapse, or continue under altered conditions.

The framework also proved capable of operating across multiple forms:

poetry,
lyric structures,
historical systems,
pedagogical models,
dramatic performance,
and recursive dialogue systems.

These developments did not replace the original framework. They emerged from it.

The chapters that follow examine how structural systems behave under increasing complexity, how thresholds operate beyond singular crossings, and how Absolute Composition functions across domains while preserving structural coherence.

The emphasis remains unchanged:
meaning emerges through arrangement,
pressure,
relation,
transformation,
and observable structural behavior.

Chapter 11

Threshold Behavior

In early formulations of Absolute Composition, thresholds were primarily understood as moments of transition between structural states.

Further compositional development revealed that thresholds do not always behave as singular crossings.

A threshold may:
accumulate,
delay,
recur,
transfer,
oscillate,
invert,
disperse,
withhold transformation,
or fail to resolve entirely.

Threshold behavior depends upon:

pressure,
containment,
duration,
distribution,
boundary condition,
and system interaction.

A threshold is therefore not merely a point of change. It is a structural condition governing how transformation behaves within a system.

Singular Thresholds

A singular threshold produces immediate transformation once pressure reaches sufficient intensity.

Examples include:
fracture under compression,
ignition under heat,
collapse under weight.

The transformation localizes clearly within the originating system.

Distributed Thresholds

A distributed threshold disperses transformation across multiple interacting regions rather than producing a singular event.

Pressure accumulates across a field until alteration emerges collectively.

Examples include:

erosion,
social unrest,
ecological saturation,
institutional instability.

Delayed Thresholds

A delayed threshold separates accumulation from visible consequence.

Transformation occurs after pressure has already exceeded stable limits.

The delay itself becomes structurally significant.

Recursive Thresholds

A recursive threshold repeatedly returns a system toward prior states while altering structural conditions with each cycle.

The system does not simply repeat.
It returns transformed.

Oscillating Thresholds

Some systems fluctuate around transformation without fully stabilizing.

The threshold remains active but unresolved.

These systems often exhibit:

feedback,
repetition,
reversal,
instability,
or suspended equilibrium.

Collapsed Thresholds

A collapsed threshold occurs when distinctions between states lose structural separability.

Boundary relations become unstable or indistinguishable.

These systems often produce:

contradiction,
indeterminacy,
identity instability,
or unresolved coexistence.

Null Thresholds

Certain systems accumulate pressure without observable transformation.

The threshold condition exists structurally even though visible consequence does not emerge.

This absence of registration remains part of the system itself.

Thresholds are therefore behavioral conditions rather than static events.

Their study requires attention not only to transformation, but to: duration, distribution, containment, recursion, and unresolved structural pressure.

Chapter 12

Structural Correspondence

Absolute Composition does not rely upon metaphor as its primary organizational principle.

Instead, it operates through structural correspondence.

Structural correspondence occurs when systems from different domains exhibit comparable organizational behavior under pressure, transformation, accumulation, distribution, or collapse.

The relationship is not symbolic resemblance.

It is behavioral equivalence.

For example:

glacial erosion and military expansion may both operate through:
accumulation,
directed pressure,
territorial reshaping,
and gradual transformation of surrounding structure.

An aquifer and an urban infrastructure system may both operate through:
storage,
channeling,
distribution,
containment,
and controlled access.

A stellar collapse and centralized authority may both exhibit:
compression,
concentration,
loss of distribution,
and singularity formation.

The compositional task is not to decorate one domain with another.

It is to identify observable structural relations shared across systems.

Because the correspondence is structural rather than symbolic:
the system remains legible even when transferred across domains.

Absolute Composition therefore treats:

natural systems,
historical systems,
social systems,
psychological systems,
linguistic systems,
and dramatic systems

as structurally comparable under certain conditions.

The integrity of the composition depends upon preserving:

behavioral accuracy,
pressure relations,
threshold coherence,
and transformational correspondence.

If the correspondence becomes merely associative or decorative, the structure weakens.

Structural correspondence is not analogy.
It is compositional equivalence through observable behavior.

Chapter 13

Structural Lyricism

Absolute Composition does not exclude lyricism.

It reorganizes the conditions through which lyric experience emerges.

In conventional lyric structures, feeling often functions as the organizing principle of the composition.

Within Absolute Composition, feeling emerges through:

relation,
pressure,
rhythm,
transformation,
residue,
recursion,
duration,
and perceptual arrangement.

The emotional field is produced structurally rather than declared symbolically.

Affect therefore becomes:
an emergent condition,
not an imposed interpretation.

Objects within the composition retain observable integrity.

Steam remains steam.
Static remains static.
Ash remains ash.
The system does not require symbolic substitution to generate resonance.

Structural lyricism often depends upon:

temporal drift,
accumulation,
aftereffect,
incomplete resolution,
echo,
and suspended transformation.

The lyric state emerges when structural pressure produces perceptual or emotional resonance across duration.

This resonance may appear as:

longing,
absence,
melancholy,
tenderness,
dread,
intimacy,
fatigue,
or uncertainty.

The composition does not explain these states.
It arranges conditions under which they emerge.

Because the lyric field remains structurally generated, the work preserves compression and observable correspondence without collapsing into sentimentality or symbolic abstraction.

Structural lyricism therefore extends Absolute Composition beyond purely operational systems while preserving the integrity of the framework itself.

Chapter 14

Dramatic Systems

Absolute Composition may operate through dramatic performance as well as through static textual structure.

Within dramatic systems, pressure unfolds behaviorally through:

dialogue,
timing,
repetition,
silence,
contradiction,
procedural escalation,
and recursive interaction.

Characters need not function primarily as psychological individuals.

They may instead operate as:

systems,
pressures,
rituals,
procedures,
belief structures,
institutional logics,
or recursive behavioral loops.

In such systems, absurdity emerges not through randomness, but through accumulation.

A logic followed beyond stable limits may produce:
contradiction,
collapse,
recursion,
displacement,
identity instability,
or unresolved repetition.

Silence functions structurally within dramatic systems.

A pause is not merely absence of speech.
It may contain:
pressure,
delay,
anticipation,
fracture,
uncertainty,
or failed transition.

Objects may also function as structural anchors within dramatic composition.

An object may accumulate pressure across the system without requiring symbolic explanation.

Repetition with variation becomes a primary mechanism of escalation.

The repeated structure gradually alters:

tone,
stability,
identity,
relation,
or logical coherence.

Blackouts within dramatic systems do not necessarily resolve the structure. They terminate it.

A dramatic threshold may therefore remain:
unfinished,
recursive,
suspended,
or behaviorally active beyond the performed scene itself.

Absolute Composition in dramatic form preserves the same foundational principles found in poetry:
compression,
structural correspondence,
observable relation,
threshold behavior,
and transformational coherence.

The difference lies in temporal enactment.
The system unfolds through performed duration.

Chapter 15

Historical Systems

Absolute Composition may also function as a method for modeling historical systems.

Rather than presenting history primarily as chronology, biography, or isolated event, the framework examines how systems:

form,
expand,
stabilize,
centralize,
accumulate pressure,
and transform under scale.

Historical structures often exhibit recurring behavioral patterns across domains.

These may include:
resource concentration,
territorial expansion,
institutional consolidation,
boundary formation,
infrastructural dependence,
economic compression,
distributed instability,
and systemic collapse.

The goal is not simplification.

The goal is structural legibility.

Through compression and correspondence, large-scale historical behavior may become observable within reduced compositional space.

Natural systems often provide structurally coherent correspondences for historical processes because both operate under:
pressure,
resource distribution,
constraint,
adaptation,
threshold behavior,
and transformation over time.

A civilization may therefore be modeled through:
erosion,
hydrology,
tectonics,
stellar collapse,
ecology,
or atmospheric systems,
provided the structural relations remain behaviorally accurate.

Historical composition within Absolute Composition does not replace historical detail.

It provides a structural framework through which large-scale systemic behavior may become perceptible.

This approach emphasizes:

cause,
pressure,
relation,
feedback,
instability,
and transformation
rather than isolated event description.

The resulting compositions function not as summaries of history,
but as compressed models of historical behavior.

Chapter 16

Cross-Form Structural Integrity

As Absolute Composition expanded across forms, a central question emerged:

What allows a structure to remain identifiable while operating within different compositional environments?

The answer is structural integrity.
A composition preserves integrity when its governing relations remain behaviorally coherent despite formal variation.

The surface form may change:

poem,
dialogue,
lyric sequence,
historical model,
dramatic performance,
instructional structure,
or recursive system.

The underlying principles remain stable:

compression,
observable relation,
threshold behavior,
pressure distribution,

structural correspondence,
and transformational coherence.

A successful cross-form composition does not imitate the surface appearance of another medium.

It preserves the behavioral architecture of the system itself.

For this reason, Absolute Composition is not defined by genre.

It is defined by:

relation,
behavior,
pressure,
and transformation.

A poem, a play, and a historical model may therefore operate within the same structural framework if their governing relations remain coherent under transformation.

The framework expands not by abandoning its principles,
but by demonstrating their persistence across increasingly varied systems.

The greater the variation,
the more important structural integrity becomes.

Without integrity,

the system dissolves into stylistic imitation or conceptual association.

With integrity,
the framework remains behaviorally recognizable across forms.

Chapter 17

Surface and Structural Approaches to Feeling

This chapter examines two different compositional approaches to feeling. The purpose is not to rank them, but to clarify structural differences.

The first example comes from a traditional lyric mode. The second comes from Absolute Composition.

A Lyrical Example

Emily Dickinson, "After great pain, a formal feeling comes—" (1862)

After great pain, a formal feeling comes—
The Nerves sit ceremonious, like Tombs—
The stiff Heart questions was it He, that bore,
And Yesterday, or Centuries before?

The Feet, mechanical, go round—
A Wooden way
Of Ground, or Air, or Ought—
Regardless grown,

A Quartz contentment, like a stone—

This is a poem about emotional aftermath. The organizing center is interior experience. The imagery—tombs, stiff heart, mechanical feet, stone —serves to articulate a psychological condition.

The poem begins with feeling ("After great pain") and develops images that interpret and intensify that feeling. Metaphor directs perception. The reader understands that "formal feeling," "nerves," "heart," and "quartz contentment" describe emotional states.

Structure supports expression.

Meaning precedes image selection.

A Structural Example

From Diction I: The Paradox of Feeling

ANGER
A tyrant—crawling on a thin-glass bridge.

In this example, the body of the poem presents a physical system. A figure of authority moves across a fragile surface. The tension arises from structural instability. The threshold is implicit: weight threatens fracture.

The title names the feeling.

The body remains observable.

There is no emotional vocabulary within the physical description. The correspondence between anger and the tyrant on glass is structural rather than explanatory.

Meaning does not precede structure. It emerges through it.

Structural Differences

In the lyrical example:

- Feeling appears first.
- Imagery serves interior articulation.
- Metaphor directs interpretation.
- The poem moves inward toward reflection.

In the structural example:

- A physical system appears first.
- The threshold organizes tension.
- Emotional language is absent from the body.
- The poem moves across a boundary condition.

The lyrical poem makes the emotional condition explicit and clarifies it through figurative language. The structural poem presents a system whose tension corresponds to the named feeling without describing it.

Both approaches engage feeling. They differ in construction.

The lyrical mode begins with experience and seeks language to express it.

Absolute Composition begins with structure and allows experience to emerge through correspondence.

One-to-One Correspondence

In both cases, anger is present.
In the lyrical poem, anger or pain is articulated internally and extended through metaphor.

In the structural poem, anger corresponds to a threshold condition: authority moving across fragility.

The feeling is not described. It is aligned with a system.

This distinction reflects two compositional logics:

- Expression-centered construction.
- Structure-centered construction.

Absolute Composition belongs to the second.

Second Comparison

Grief / Pain

Lyrical Example:
Emily Dickinson, "I measure every Grief I meet" (public domain)

I measure every Grief I meet
With narrow, probing, eyes—
I wonder if It weighs like Mine—
Or has an Easier size.

This poem organizes itself around interior comparison. The speaker encounters grief in others and measures it against personal experience. The emotional condition is explicit. The imagery and structure serve introspection.

Grief is the organizing center.
Image functions as interpretive extension.
Meaning precedes structure.

The poem moves inward.

Structural Example

From Diction I: The Paradox of Feeling

ANXIETY
Cracked glacier—
a sinking floating iceberg.

In this example, the body presents a physical instability: fracture and displacement within a frozen system.

The threshold lies in the paradox of floating mass that is simultaneously sinking. The triad may be understood as solid / fracture / descent.

The title names the feeling.

The poem does not describe anxiety. It presents a system under tension.

The reader encounters instability rather than confession.

Structural Contrast

In Dickinson:

- Grief is articulated directly.
- The poem examines emotional measurement.
- The speaker is central.
- Metaphor clarifies feeling.

In the structural poem:

- The physical system is central.
- The threshold generates tension.
- No speaker appears.
- Emotional language is absent from the body.

Both address interior instability.
One interprets it.
The other aligns it with structure.

Third Comparison

Hope

For this comparison, we move from Feeling to Faith, since hope bridges both.

Lyrical Example

Emily Dickinson, "Hope is the thing with feathers" (public domain)

"Hope" is the thing with feathers—
That perches in the soul—
And sings the tune without the words—
And never stops—at all—

This poem personifies hope as a bird. The metaphor is explicit and sustained. The emotional abstraction becomes an image that carries reassurance.

Hope is defined through metaphor.
The poem interprets and comforts.
Image serves expression.

Structural Example

From Diction II: The Paradox of Faith

HOPE

Godwit—
shrunk livers—
callow,

flapping over rivers,
slivers—

a gurgling mud pot—
hissing.

Benediction: Move, uncertainly.

Here, the poem presents a migratory shorebird system under strain. The emphasis is on movement, vulnerability, and endurance across unstable terrain.

The threshold is migration itself: departure across uncertainty.

Hope is not described as comfort. It is aligned with precarious motion.

The body remains physical.
The title names the condition.
The benediction offers structural orientation rather than explanation.

Structural Contrast

In Dickinson:

- Hope is metaphorically defined.
- The poem reassures.
- Emotional abstraction drives imagery.
- Meaning is interpretively guided.

In the structural poem:

- Hope corresponds to migratory threshold.
- Movement replaces reassurance.
- The physical system carries tension.
- Interpretation is not directed.

Both poems address hope.
One conceptualizes it through metaphor.
The other aligns it with threshold and motion.

What These Three Comparisons Clarify

Across Anger, Anxiety / Grief, and Hope:

Lyrical Mode:

- Begins with feeling.
- Uses metaphor to interpret.
- Centers interior voice.
- Moves toward reflection or reassurance.

Absolute Composition:

- Begins with a physical system.
- Identifies a threshold.
- Maintains structural compression.

- Allows correspondence without explanation.

This is the one-to-one correspondence you described:

A book that does feelings through surface articulation.
A book that does feelings through structural depth.

They are not oppositional.

They are differently constructed.

Expanded Structural Comparison

Hope and Triadic Organization

Lyrical Example

Emily Dickinson, "Hope is the thing with feathers"

"Hope" is the thing with feathers—
That perches in the soul—
And sings the tune without the words—
And never stops—at all—

Structural Observation

This poem organizes hope metaphorically as a bird.

We can identify an implicit triad operating within the lyric:

Bird / Song / Storm

Across the poem, hope:

- Perches (stability)
- Sings (continuity)
- Endures storms (adversity)

The threshold appears in moments of extremity:

"In the Gale"
"And sore must be the storm"

The crossing occurs when conditions worsen. The song persists despite the storm.

However, the triad functions symbolically rather than structurally.

Bird = Hope
Song = Comfort
Storm = Difficulty

The middle term (song) mediates between hope and adversity. It stabilizes the system emotionally. The triad resolves tension by reassurance.

The structure supports metaphor. The metaphor carries meaning.

Structural Example

From Diction II: The Paradox of Faith

HOPE

Godwit—
shrunk livers—
callow,

flapping over rivers,
slivers—

a gurgling mud pot—
hissing.

Benediction: Move, uncertainly.

Structural Mapping

The poem presents a migratory shorebird under stress.

We can map the triad explicitly:

Departure / Migration / Landing

Or more precisely within the physical system:

Shrinking fuel reserves / Flight / Uncertain terrain

The threshold is migration itself — the crossing from one geographic state to another.

Unlike Dickinson's lyric, the middle term does not stabilize. It destabilizes.

Migration is risk.
Movement exposes vulnerability.
Hope is aligned with motion across danger.

The triad does not resolve tension. It sustains it.

There is no metaphor equating hope with bird. Instead, hope corresponds structurally to migratory threshold.

The bird is not "like" hope. The system shares its pattern.

Direct Triad Comparison

Dickinson:

Hope (bird)
↓
Song
↓
Storm

The middle term (song) protects and reassures.
Tension resolves into endurance.

Structural Hope:

Fuel depletion
↓
Flight (threshold)
↓
Precarious terrain

The middle term (migration) intensifies exposure.
Tension remains active.

What This Reveals

In the lyrical mode:

- The triad serves metaphor.
- The middle term mediates and comforts.
- The threshold confirms emotional resilience.
- Meaning is guided.

In Absolute Composition:

- The triad organizes transformation.
- The middle term is a structural threshold.
- The threshold sustains tension.
- Meaning emerges from correspondence.

Both poems treat hope.

One defines it through metaphor and assurance. The other aligns it with a system under strain.

The difference lies not in subject but in construction.

Chapter 18

Structural Visibility in Instruction

Absolute Composition clarifies several recurring challenges in poetry instruction by shifting attention from interpretive speculation to structural observation. The method does not eliminate interpretation; it sequences it. Construction becomes visible first. Interpretation may follow.

1. From Interpretive Decoding to Structural Observation

In many classrooms, poems are approached as puzzles requiring interpretive decoding. Students search for hidden meaning before identifying how the poem is built.

Absolute Composition reverses that order. Because arrangement generates meaning and interpretation does not govern construction, students begin by identifying transformation: the initial state, the threshold, and the resulting condition. Discussion stabilizes around what is structurally present before expanding into inference.

2. Reducing Interpretive Pressure Through Observable Systems

Students often experience poetry as high-stakes interpretation. The demand to "understand what it means" can produce hesitation or withdrawal.

By grounding composition in observable physical systems—fracture, phase change, pressure, growth, migration—the method anchors discussion in publicly verifiable conditions. Students articulate what happens structurally rather than speculate about what is intended. The poem becomes examinable rather than mysterious.

3. Moving Beyond Personal Mirroring

When classroom discussion centers on relatability, poems may be valued primarily for autobiographical alignment.

Structural correspondence provides a different entry point. A physical system and a psychological condition may share pattern without sharing narrative. Students examine transformation rather than personal identification. The poem's architecture becomes the bridge.

4. Clarifying Assessment Through Structural Criteria

Interpretation varies. Structural construction does not.

Because Absolute Composition centers on transformation, threshold, register, and compression, evaluation can focus on structural integrity:

- Is the transformation perceptible?
- Is the threshold concentrated?
- Are the registers distinct?
- Does compression intensify or diffuse the system?

Assessment becomes transparent. Students understand what is being evaluated and why.

5. Structural Emphasis in Context

Absolute Composition does not replace interpretive approaches. It clarifies construction before interpretation. Where some instructional models foreground expression or symbolic substitution, this method foregrounds transformation and structural relation.

Triad as Metaphor vs. Triad as Structure

The comparisons above reveal an important distinction. Both lyrical poetry and Absolute Composition often rely on triadic organization. The difference lies in how the triad functions.

Triad as Metaphor

In the lyrical mode, the triad often operates symbolically. One element stands for an emotional state, and the remaining elements extend or clarify that state.

In Dickinson's "Hope is the thing with feathers," the triadic structure can be traced through:

Bird / Song / Storm

The bird represents hope.
The song represents its persistence.
The storm represents adversity.

The triad is metaphorical. Its elements are not independent systems but symbolic carriers of emotional meaning. The middle term mediates tension. The song persists through the storm, reinforcing reassurance. The structure resolves into affirmation.

In this mode:

- Feeling precedes image.
- The triad clarifies interior experience.
- The middle term stabilizes.

- Interpretation is directed.

The triad serves expression.

Triad as Structure

In Absolute Composition, the triad emerges from an observable system. It is not assigned symbolic meaning. It organizes transformation across a threshold.

In the structural example of hope from Diction II , the triad may be mapped as:

Fuel depletion / Migration / Arrival terrain

These elements are not symbols for hope. They are conditions within a physical system. The middle term—migration—is a threshold state. It intensifies exposure rather than resolving it.

The tension remains active because the triad reflects real transformation. The poem does not interpret the system; it presents it.

In this mode:

- Structure precedes interpretation.
- The triad organizes state change.
- The middle term marks a threshold.
- Meaning emerges through correspondence.

The triad serves construction.

Structural Implications

When a triad functions metaphorically, it translates feeling into image. The reader understands the emotional content through symbolic alignment.

When a triad functions structurally, it traces transformation within a system. The reader encounters tension through observable change.

Both approaches employ three-part organization. The distinction lies in sequence and function.

Metaphorical triad:
Feeling → Image → Resolution.

Structural triad:
State → Threshold → New state.

The subject may remain the same—anger, grief, hope—but the compositional logic differs.

Absolute Composition does not remove feeling from poetry. It relocates it. The emotional condition is not narrated; it corresponds to a structural transformation.

The triad becomes not an illustration, but an engine.

Afterword

Absolute Composition begins with observation and develops through threshold. It relies on triadic tension and compression to sustain structure.

The comparison with music clarifies its foundation. In absolute music, motif develops through harmonic instability and returns altered or reaffirmed. No narrative explanation is required. The structure carries the experience.

In poetry, the medium changes, but the principle remains consistent. A physical system crosses a threshold. A triad organizes tension. Compression removes excess. The poem holds its shape through transformation.

Feeling is not excluded. It is aligned structurally rather than described directly. The reader encounters change rather than commentary.

Across the chapters of this book, the method has been presented as construction rather than persuasion. It does not replace other approaches to poetry. It demonstrates one way of organizing language so that structure generates meaning.

In both music and poetry, the threshold is where attention concentrates. Before the threshold, one state holds. After it, another does. The crossing is perceptible.

When the transformation remains clear and the structure remains intact, the composition is complete.

Structure holds.

Glossary of Terms

FOUNDATIONAL TERMS

Absolute Composition
A structural compositional framework organized through compression, observable relation, threshold behavior, correspondence, and transformation rather than symbolic substitution alone.

Behavior
The manner in which a system transforms, stabilizes, distributes pressure, recurs, collapses, or persists under structural conditions.

Boundary
A structural limit regulating containment, transfer, reflection, filtration, accumulation, or transformation between systems.

Compression
The reduction of language or structure to the minimum necessary for preserving relational and transformational integrity.

Containment
The condition through which pressure, material, energy, or structural relation remains held within a system or boundary.

Correspondence
A structural relation between systems based upon shared behavior rather than symbolic resemblance.

Observable Relation
A perceptible structural interaction between systems, materials, conditions, or transformations.

Pressure
Accumulated force, tension, instability, contradiction, or transformational potential within a system.

Recursion
The return of a system, structure, or condition in altered or repeated form across duration.

Structural Integrity
The preservation of governing relational coherence within a composition despite variation or expansion.

Threshold
A structural condition governing transformation between states, systems, relations, or behaviors.

Transformation
A structural alteration produced through pressure, relation, duration, accumulation, or threshold behavior.

Triad
A three-part structural relation organizing transformation, correspondence, or compositional interaction.

THRESHOLD BEHAVIOR

Collapsed Threshold
A threshold condition in which distinctions between states lose structural separability, producing instability or unresolved coexistence.

Delayed Threshold
A threshold in which observable transformation emerges after pressure has already exceeded stable limits.

Distributed Threshold
A threshold condition whose transformation disperses across multiple interacting systems or regions rather than localizing at a singular point.

Null Threshold
A threshold condition in which pressure accumulates without visible registration or observable transformation.

Oscillating Threshold
A threshold condition in which a system fluctuates around transformation without fully stabilizing.

Recursive Threshold
A threshold that repeatedly returns a system toward prior states while altering structural conditions with each cycle.

Singular Threshold
A threshold producing immediate and localized transformation once pressure reaches sufficient intensity.

STRUCTURAL CORRESPONDENCE

Behavioral Equivalence
Similarity between systems based upon comparable transformational behavior rather than thematic resemblance.

Cross-Domain Relation
A structural correspondence operating coherently across distinct systems such as natural, historical, dramatic, social, or linguistic forms.

Structural Correspondence
Behavioral equivalence between systems across domains grounded in shared structural relations rather than symbolic analogy.

STRUCTURAL LYRICISM

Emergent Affect
Emotional or perceptual resonance produced through arrangement, duration, transformation, pressure, and relation rather than direct declaration.

Residual State
A lingering structural condition persisting after primary transformation has occurred.

Structural Lyricism
A compositional condition in which affective resonance emerges through structural relation rather than symbolic or confessional organization.

DRAMATIC SYSTEMS

Procedural Absurdity
Absurdity generated through accumulation and rigid continuation of internal logic rather than randomness or exaggeration.

Recursive Escalation
The gradual intensification of pressure through repetition with variation.

Structural Silence
A pause functioning as active pressure, delay, instability, anticipation, or suspended transformation within a dramatic system.

HISTORICAL SYSTEMS

Historical Compression
The reduction of large-scale historical behavior into structurally legible compositional systems.

Structural History
An approach to historical modeling emphasizing pressure, transformation, infrastructure, accumulation, and systemic relation over isolated event narration.

Systemic Concentration
The accumulation of pressure, authority, dependency, or structural force into increasingly centralized formations.

CROSS-FORM TERMS

Cross-Form Integrity
The preservation of structural coherence across differing compositional forms.

Structural Persistence
The continuation of governing relational principles despite variation in surface form, medium, or compositional environment.

Appendix

Structural Applications

The following examples demonstrate how Absolute Composition may operate across differing compositional forms while preserving structural integrity.

The purpose of these demonstrations is not interpretive explanation. It is structural observation. Each example organizes transformation through:

pressure,
relation,
threshold behavior,
correspondence,
and observable change.

The forms differ. The governing structural principles remain coherent.

I. Poetic Compression

Ice on the railing—
sunlight—
dripping,
dark stain spreading
through cedar grain.

Structural Behavior:
containment → exposure → transfer

The transformation emerges through observable pressure and material interaction rather than symbolic declaration.

The system remains compressed while preserving threshold clarity.

II. Structural Lyricism

Steam lifting
from the untouched cup—
radio static
through the apartment wall.

Structural Behavior:
absence → residue → persistence

The composition produces emotional resonance through arrangement, duration, and residual condition rather than direct emotional statement.

III. Historical Compression

Aqueduct—
stone channels
crossing dry valleys—
city swelling
behind the hills.

Structural Behavior:
resource → distribution → concentration

The historical system is modeled through infrastructure, accumulation, and structural expansion rather than chronological narration.

IV. Dramatic Recursion

A: Did you move the chair?

B: No.

A: Then why is it facing the wall?

B: Maybe it prefers the wall.

A: Chairs do not prefer things.

B: Then why has it remained there all morning?

Structural Behavior:
question → contradiction → escalation

Pressure accumulates through recursive logic and procedural continuation rather than through external conflict.

V. Cross-Form Structural Integrity

Structural Sequence:
accumulation → saturation → collapse

Poetic Form:
Rainwater pooling
at the basement steps—
soil slipping inward.

Dramatic Form:
Three speakers continue talking simultaneously until none can distinguish their own sentences.

Historical Form:
Administrative expansion exceeds the infrastructure required to maintain coordination across regions.

Lyric Form:
Unanswered messages gathering across weeks—
screen glow
in the dark room.

Across forms, the governing structure remains behaviorally coherent despite changes in surface presentation.

The framework persists through relation rather than genre.

Acknowledgments

This book developed alongside a body of poems built through practice. Over time, certain structural principles became consistent enough to describe. The work owes its clarity to repeated drafting, revision, and sustained attention to observable systems.

Gratitude is extended to the students, teachers, and readers who engaged with these poems in classrooms and workshops. Their questions and responses helped clarify the vocabulary used here.

Thanks also to colleagues and early readers who encouraged the documentation of this method. Their insistence on precision strengthened the structure of this book.

About the Author

J. A. Gucci is a writer, structural theorist, and educator whose work explores compression, threshold behavior, transformation, and cross-form systems within literary and compositional practice.

He developed the framework of Absolute Composition, a structural method grounded in observable relation rather than symbolic substitution. His work examines how pressure, correspondence, recursion, containment, accumulation, transfer, and transformation operate across poetic, dramatic, historical, pedagogical, and conceptual systems.

His published works include:
Metaphysical Unfolds,
Philosophical Unfolds,
Structural Lyricism,
Twelve Roman Thresholds,
and The Human Error Plays.

Across these works, he investigates how structural behavior may generate meaning through arrangement, relation, and transformation rather than through interpretive abstraction alone.

He lives and works in the United States.

Colophon

This volume was composed according to the principles of Absolute Composition, a structural framework organized through compression, correspondence, threshold behavior, and observable transformation.

The text was designed to preserve clarity of structural relation across multiple compositional forms, including poetry, lyric systems, historical modeling, dramatic systems, and pedagogical structures.

Typography and spacing were intentionally constrained to emphasize pressure, pacing, recursion, suspension, accumulation, and release. Lineation and sectional arrangement were treated as structural mechanisms rather than decorative elements.

Part I presents the foundational principles of the framework as originally formulated.

Part II documents later developments that emerged through continued compositional practice and cross-form application.

No ornamental elements were included beyond those necessary for structural separation, legibility, and compositional coherence.

Composed and structurally refined in the United States.

Second Expanded Edition, 2026.

Printed by Libri Plureos GmbH in Hamburg,
Germany

9 798994 675199